Picture Poems
Volume 2

Thomas G. Reischel

Word Art Publishing
9350 Wilshire Blvd
Suite 203, Beverly Hills, CA 90212
www.wordartpublishing.com
Phone: 1 (888) 614 - 1370

Published by Word Art Publishing

ISBN: 978-1-955070-71-3 (Hardcover)
ISBN: 978-1-955070-60-7 (Paperback)
ISBN: 978-1-955070-61-4 (eBook)

DEDICATION

· ·

*To my brothers and sisters, who believed
in me, and all poetry lovers everywhere.*

INTRODUCTION

. . . .

After the success of Volume 1, I have found it delightful to continue on with another series of the poems stimulated by the pictures and visa-versa. In Volume 2, I have included two new categories that weren't found in Volume 1. These are: Autumn/Spring, and Pathways. Still, the two largest categories of poems in this volume , with 12 each, fall under the categories of Birds and Scenes. Both are areas of deep passion for me. I can't wait to lead you to those gems. But first, I'll begin with a discussion of my purpose and a short poetry primer. If you read my previous volumes, you have already seen this before. If not, here it is.

I believe that photography and poetry go together well. One form paints a visual picture while the other creates a poetic image. Together, the synergy becomes very powerful. At least, that is what I hope I have achieved here. This book contains both. All the photographs contained in this book were taken by the author and the poetry was also written by him.

The author resides in St. Paul, Minnesota, USA. The photos were all taken within the state. So, besides the esthetic visual journey, he hopes the book also provides the reader a bit of information about the place that is his home.

Besides the poem itself, the author will typically add author's notes. These notes generally try to provide three bits of information. First will be a comment about the poem itself. Second, a description of the poetic format is provided. Finally, the author may comment about the photograph. This is provided to be informational. It may be redundant or unnecessary for some. Those individuals can skip over what they want, part or even all of the notes. They are there for those who want them.

So, this book is really meant for several types of readers. There will be those who merely want to see the photographs. I think that is wonderful, and hope that my photography is sufficiently good enough to satisfy their craving. Others will just like the poetry. Again, although I don't purport to be an expert, I hope that I have at least accomplished some success and have whetted their appetite for more. Some may want to focus on style and format, and I believe this book should appeal to them as well.

The chapters have been organized by the category of photograph for the picture lovers, then in alphabetical order of the poem's title. There are chapters with Animal/Wildlife, Birds, Flowers, Gardens, Sunrise and Sunsets to please the eye.

The author doesn't claim to be an authority in these areas, so please allow him a bit of poetic license.

For those, who are new to poetry, I need to give a bit of information that may help you understand poetry better. This is necessary because I refer to these standard forms of poetic schematics frequently within my author's notes. So this section is intended to help a reader grasp the references adequately, not to be a detailed poetry education. This is fairly technical, but I'll try to explain it as simply as possible. I didn't invent this system; it has been around a long time. I am merely going to explain some of it to you here. Those who are already familiar can skip this part of the introduction, unless you feel you need a refresher.

Poetry comes in many styles and forms. My poems identify what the style it is meant to be. Let's start with a discussion of rhyme. Poems may or may not have rhyme. The rhyme is usually at the end of each line and is known as "end rhyme". If not at the end, it is known as "in-line rhyme". As you read my poetic descriptions, I may refer to the end rhymes in an alphanumeric code. For example, the first rhyming word in a poem is referred to as the "a" rhyme, and every line in the poem that rhymes with it is designated the letter "a". The second rhyme to occur would be identified as "b", the third as "c", and so on. The most common poem has 4 lines (a Quatrain). The most typical end rhyme schemes for a quatrain are:

aabb (Coupled Rhyme)
abab (Alternating Rhyme)
abba (Enveloping Ryme)
abcb (Skipping Rhyme)

Poems may contain a paragraph. These are known as stanzas. These stanzas may contain the same rhyme or may vary. Here are examples of the rhyme scheme of a poem with two stanzas.

aabb baba (Here the rhyme was the same in both, but one was coupled while the other was alternating).

aabb ccdd (Here each stanza has two different coupled rhymes).

Poems may also contain one or more repeating rhyme. That means it has the same identical rhyme word. This is usually identified using a capital letter, like so:

Abab Abab (Here I'm referring to the first line of each stanza).

It could also mean a complete repeating line or refrain. That would be identified in the author's notes.

Poems may also have varying numbers of lines. Here is a list of the most common:

Couplet: 2 Lines
Tercet: 3 Lines
Quatrain: 4 lines
Quintet: 5 Lines
Sestet: 6 Lines

Poems can also mix stanza styles. For example, a Sonnet usually contains 3 quatrains and a couplet (14 total lines).

Poems also may contain a structured syllable count. This establishes the rhythm at which the poem is read. This is known as meter. Typically these are paired in sets of two, known as a foot. There is a name for each type of meter, as follows.

Two syllables - Monometer (one foot)
Four syllables - Dimeter (two feet)
Six syllables - Trimeter (three feet)
Eight syllables - Tetrameter (four feet)
Ten syllables - Pentameter (five feet)
Twelve syllables - Hexameter (six feet)
Fourteen syllables - Heptameter (seven feet)
Sixteen Syllables - Octameter (eight feet)

The ones most common or frequently used are tetrameter and pentameter.

The most complex poetic concept focuses around syllable accents, whether they are hard or soft, and how they are linked together. The most common of these are iambic and the trochaic (trochee) meters. As you speak a word, there is an accent on each syllable that results in either a soft or a hard sound. For example the word cowboy puts the hard accent on the first syllable – **COW**boy. The word police, puts the hard accent on the second syllable – po**LICE**. How you string words together determines the type of meter. Iambic meter alternates soft -hard, soft- hard. For example, Shakespeare's famous words –"To be or not to be" is iambic: to **BE** or **NOT** to **BE**. But the second half is not iambic – **THAT** is the **QUES**tion. Iambic is frequently defined as da-Dum, da-DUM type meter, where each da-Dum is a poetic foot. Therefore, iambic pentameter would carry a meter of: da-**DUM**, da-**DUM**, da-**Dum**, da-**DUM**, da-**DUM**. Trochee is exactly the opposite of iambic, where each line starts with a hard syllable accent and ends with a soft. **TWIN**kle **TWIN**kle **LIT**tle **STAR** how **I** won**DER** what **YOU** are.

Well, that's about all I want to get into on rhyme and meter, but I do want to discuss poetic technique a bit.

In volume 2, I added some more detail than I had in volume 1. For each poem, I listed in detail some of the poetic techniques employed, such as: alliteration, assonance, and in-line rhyming. I hope readers will appreciate my pointing these things out as it is not my intention to bore them, but rather I hope it may bring additional depth of appreciation to the poetry. If not, feel free to skip over that part.

Here is a description of a few poetic techniques available.

Alliteration: The use of repetitive first letters (usually consonants) at the beginning of words. Often these words are consecutive, but don't necessarily need to be. Alliteration occurs when the same letters (or sound, such as ph and f) are repeated more than once in a line of poetry. In a structured poem, such as one with quatrains or couplets, the distinction of what constitutes a line is pretty clear. Below is an example of alliteration used in a couplet in poem 41, Cherub Fountain and poem 40, Casting Shadows, where the poetic line is pretty clear.

(From poem 41)

> Yon cherubs *dance delightfully* in sky.
> These little water nymphs *pleasantly play*

(From poem 40)

> *Watchers* don't *want* the *scene* to end too *soon*.
> It's amazing, when that *golden* orb *glows*.

It's a bit different in a Free Verse poem, where the line is not as distinct. There, the alliteration occurs within a phrase or completed thought. Below is an example of alliteration within a Free Verse from poem 49, The Pond.

> Then I turned a corner
> and
> *beheld*
> a **wooden** *bench*
> *beside* the sparkling **water**.

Assonance: The repetition of similar vowel sounds within a line of poetry, but not at the beginning of the words. Below is an example of the assonance expressed by the U sound in a line from poem 29, Silken Swirls.

> Rich the *hues* this *bush imbues*,

Consonance: The repetition of similar consonant sounds within a line of poetry, but not at the beginning of the words. This line from poem 12, Baltimore Orioles provides an example of the consonance created by the TW sound.

> Sitting *twixt the twigs*, raising spirits high,

In-line Rhyme: Where one or more rhymes occur within a line of poetry, rather than between lines. The rhyme may match the end-rhyme, or any other word in that line, or both. The following lines from poem 15, The Coot's Call, is an example. The in-line rhyme is on the first line below. "Great" rhymes with the end-line rhyme "fate", which rhymes with "mate".

> The chance is *great*; he'll find love's *fate*.
> In tall swamp grass a Coot did hide,
> So lonely, looking for a mate.

Onomatopoeia: This is the use of words that denote a sound or the feel of a sound. For example, "Oink" is the sound made by a pig. "Swish" isn't a sound, but gives the feel of a sound. An example comes from poem 43, Fido on the Roof.

> Looked across the street this morning,
> There was a doggy on the roof.

The surprise came without warning
When I was startled by a *"woof"*.

Anaphora: The repeated use of a word or phrase at the beginning of a phrase, line, or stanza, that provides an impact or to underline a point in poetry, or speeches for that matter. The most famous use of Anaphora was "I have a dream", by Martin Luther King Jr. For an example of this technique, see poem 14, Comes the Muse.

Caesura: A pause or stop in a line of poetry, usually with some form of punctuation.

There are several other techniques, but these are the major ones that I wanted to address here. Volume 3 will address some more.

This concludes the Introduction to Volume 2. I welcome you to join me with this next set of 50 poems. Hope you enjoy them immensely. I certainly enjoyed writing them.

ACKNOWLEDGEMENTS

. . . .

I'd like to recognize and thank my understanding wife, Karen Lynne (Sweetnam) Reischel, for providing support by reading all my poems as they were created and making helpful suggestions, as well as being the final editor. I'd also like to thank all my FanStory friends and fans who also helped and encouraged me. Finally, the staff at Word Art Publishing who provided their valuable assistance, especially Beau Brandon whose patience and persuasion over several years has gotten me here. Thank you all for your time and effort. For without it, this book could never have been possible.

TABLE OF CONTENTS

CHAPTER 1: AUTUMN/SPRING

· ·

Who doesn't find the burst of new life in the Spring, or the fantastic colors of Autumn, inspiring? Certainly they are both candidates for the photographer's eye and the poet's pen. I really enjoy getting out the camera bags and lenses to capture the images. Those images fascinate my muse and drive it to create flowing verse. Here in these pages, I have tried to capture the essence of both. I hope that you agree.

Poem #1:

A GOLDEN ALLEY
(Mixed Formats)

<<Triolet>>

Take me down this golden alley
That leads me to a large stone church,
Where the sinners seldom sally.
Take me down this golden alley
Where the leaves of Autumn dally
With all the maples and the birch.
Take me down this golden alley
That leads me to a large stone church.

<<Minute Poem>>

That's where I want to go, you know,
In golden glow,
With cobbled streets,
And vined retreats.

There's so much earthy comfort there,
In open air,
The breeze is crisp,
With windy wisp.

The serenity of this path,
Reduces wrath,
As one can see,
Most avidly.

<<5-7-5>>

This golden alley
Where leaves of autumn dally
My spirits rally

This golden alley leads to the Cathedral of St. Paul in Minnesota. The autumn colors on the trees and vines climbing the buildings made such a lovely sight, I was inspired to write this poem.

This poem contains three separate poetic formats: a Triolet, a Minute Poem, and a 5-7-5 Poem.

A Triolet is a poem of only eight lines with a rhyme scheme ABaAabAB. The fourth and seventh lines are the same exact line as the first. The eighth line is the same exact line as the second.

The Minute Poem is a poem that follows the "8,4,4,4" syllable count structure. It usually has 3 stanzas that are exactly the same. So: 8,4,4,4; 8,4,4,4; 8,4,4,4 syllables.

A traditional Minute Poem has 12 lines total. It has 60 syllables. It is written in a strict iambic meter. The rhyme scheme is as follows: aabb, ccdd, eeff.

A 5-7-5 follows the structure of a Haiku. See Poem 34, Sits in Sand, for a discussion about a Haiku. It has three lines. The first line has 5 syllables. The second line has 7 syllables. The third line has 5 syllables again.

Alliteration: leads large, sinners seldom sally, where want, golden glow, with windy wisp.

Assonance: the O sounds in "to go you know", the I sound in "in air".

Consonance: the S sound in "is crisp".

In-line Rhyme: go you know.

Caesura: That's where I want to go, you know.

This photograph was taken by the author on October, 2012 at St. Paul, MN. in the alley adjacent to the Cathedral's parking lot.

Poem #2:

AN AUTUMN SCENE
(Blank Verse)

I'm thinking lovely thoughts of fall,
Complete with color red on leaves
Still hung on young new maple trees.

As willows gauntly weep with wind,
They wait while geese pick summer seed,
their bellies full from dormant grass.

Alive in crisp brisk autumn air,
They're out there where once picnics were,
To get them set for flying south.

Oh, such sweet season's rich tableau,
This smart sight, silently is sought,
For view by poet's passive eye.

This pastoral fall scene spoke to me of the leaves changing and geese getting ready to fly south.

This poem is a Blank Verse.

A Blank Verse poem is written without rhymes. It does have a set metrical pattern, usually iambic pentameter. But it is a flexible form that is often used in narrative and dramatic poetry. It was popularized by William Shakespeare.

I formatted the poem, as each verse is a Tercet.

This poem does also use a bit of alliteration in several lines and other poetic techniques.

In-line rhyme: get set, hung young, there where.

Alliteration: complete color, willows weep with wind, wait while, summer seed, full from, alive autumn air, where were, for flying, such sweet season's, smart sight silently is sought, poet's passive, by eye.

Assonance: the O sounds in "lovely thoughts of".

Consonance: the R sound of "dormant grass", the mimicked W sound in "once were".

Caesura: see lines 10 and 11.

This photograph was taken by the author at Lake Phalen in St. Paul, Minnesota during October 2012 along the lagoon.

Poem #3:

AUTUMN'S DECK
(A Rubiyat Poem)

Where I oft' sit, I spot some leaves,
To Adirondack's seat each cleaves.
Invading too my private deck,
That Autumn's artist's touch achieves.

I love the feelings they invoke,
When nature adds its master stroke,
That's always different when I check,
As all the changing trees uncloak.

This season adds a crisp cool breeze,
Foretelling Winter's coming freeze.
I'll just throw on my turtleneck,
Before I catch a nasty sneeze.

Now I'll go out to sit awhile,
And brush away that leafy pile,
To marvel at each color fleck,
Complete with coffee and a smile.

The leaves are starting to fall as my Adirondack chair assumes the look of fall.

This poetic format was introduced to me by Gungalo, a poet on Fanstory.com.

Rubiyat: this Arabic format has a quatrain wherein the first, second, and fourth lines rhyme.

The rhyme scheme is thus; a-a-b-a.

A single stanza can be a poem in itself or multiple stanzas may be joined to create a larger piece. Eight syllables per line. I also rhymed the third line of the first stanza with the third line of every stanza, but that is not a requirement. So, the rhyme scheme for this particular poem is:

aaba ccbc ddbd eebe.

Alliteration: sit spot some, Autumn's artist achieves, crisp cool, throw turtleneck, and complete coffee.

Assonance: of EA sound in "seat each cleaves", the A sound in "as all", the O sound in "throw on", the O sound "now go out to", the A sound in "at each".

Consonance: the T sound in "artist's touch", the S sound in "nasty sneeze", the W sound in "now awhile", and the L sound in "color fleck."

Caesura: line 1.

I took this picture out my back deck, October 24, 2013.

Poem #4:

BUDS BEGIN TO SHOW
(Rondeau Redouble)

As buds begin to show on trees
Their promise stirs my sour soul.
Bare branches dangle in the breeze,
They whisper, "Spring is in control".

The limbs that grace my favorite knoll
Have shaken off the winter's freeze.
They have begun their Summer role
As buds begin to show on trees.

At last the Angels answered pleas,
The Winter blues are on parole.
As proof, new birth my vision sees,
Their promise stirs my sour soul.

The new found freshness makes me whole
To promised pulse of God's decrees.
I gaze amazed here as I stroll,
Bare branches dangle in the breeze.

As new growth brushes 'gainst my knees
To greet God's splendor is my goal.
Amongst returning birds and bees,
They whisper, "Spring is in control".

Nature's bounty will soon unroll.
So grab those treasures you can seize,
And seek those finds that you'll extol
As buds begin to show on trees.

Thoughts of spring abound as the trees and other plants begin to bud. I spotted this budding bush in the woods. I loved the criss-cross pattern it made with those lovely red branches.

This poem is a Rondeau Redouble.

The Rondeau Redouble is not, as its name suggests, a double Rondeau. With a strict rhyming pattern it consists of six stanzas (quatrains) and a final refrain, all on two rhymes. Each line of the first stanza becomes, in turn, the last line of the four succeeding stanzas. The sixth stanza is all new though followed by the first phrase of the first line.

For this poem I've chosen a syllable count of 8.

In addition to a rich texture of alliteration used in this poem, I also included assonance, where two similar words appear in the same line, for example: I gaze amazed.

The rhyme scheme is: abab.

Alliteration: buds begin, stirs sour soul, bare branches breeze, Angels answered, found freshness, promised pulse, greet God's goal, birds bees, those treasures.

Assonance: the O sound in "to show on", the I sound in "is in", the A sound in "have shaken", the U sound in "begun summer".

Consonance: the S sound in "promise stirs" and "Spring is".

In-line rhyme: gaze amazed.

Caesura: see line 4, and line 11.

This photograph was taken by the author in the spring of 2011.

Poem #5:

CROWN OF LEAVES

(Free Verse)

As I looked
in astonishment
at
the silent sky

Transfixed
by
the fluttering leaves.
The arching branches
caught my eye
with
their colors of
red and green.

Their graceful forms,
so light
and free
in
the forest
air.
Wrought
a
wonderful screen,
forming
a marvelous shape
in
the form of
a
Crown of Leaves
with
its central curves.

Revealing
an image of
The Heart
in the Tree.

Can you see the heart? It's formed by the branches and the leaves.

In Southwestern Minnesota along the Great Plains region of the state is Shetek State Park. In August of 2012, I took this photograph of a flowering tree that was located right in the middle of the Campground. The leaves and branches looked like they formed a beautiful heart in the middle. That tickled my romantic Muse and inspired me to write this little free verse poem.

I wrote this in Free Verse.

A Free Verse poem has no format, rhyme scheme, or structure. The words themselves express the emotions as the author sets the pace and pause in the manner the words are laid out.

Capitalization intended for impact.

Alliteration: as astonishment at, silent sky, by branches, caught color, forms free forest, central curves, wrought wonderful, the the tree.

Assonance: the A sound in "arching branches", the O sound in "colors of", the E sound in "red green".

Consonance: the T sound in "astonishment at", the R sound in "arching branches", the V sound in "curves revealing".

In-line rhyme: my eye.

Onomatopoeia: fluttering.

This photograph is the reason that this poem exists. It moved me to express what I saw in verse.

Poem #6:

FALL'S FORCE
(A 5A Poem)

Leaves leave lasting look
Lay low letting loose
Feeling fall's full force

Yellow leaves on Maple tree. Some still have a hint of green in them, while others are turning a leathery brown. Two days later, they dropped.

This is a 5A poem.

The "5A" new format style was developed by Fanstorian DRG24.

*The 5A is composed of three lines:

Line 1 - 5 Syllables

Line 2 - 5 Syllables

Line 3 - 5 Syllables

All lines must have TOTAL alliteration. Lines can be chosen in any order. However, the alliteration may either be identical throughout the poem, or may vary from line to line.

The "5" stands for the five syllable count while the "A" stands for the Alliteration.

Here, I chose the use of alliteration of L in the first 2 lines, but then changed to F in the third.

Used an interesting conjunction of Homonyms (Leaves leave), which are two words that are spelled and pronounced the same, but mean different things.

This picture was taken by the author in October 2013, at Battle Creek Park in Maplewood, MN.

Poem #7:

ROADSIDE REDS
(A Minute Poem)

On Autumn ride, bound to collide,
Somewhere outside,
With roadside reds
In color spreads.

Then you'll spot a touch of yellow
Hues that mellow
Peaking behind
Branches entwined.

Deciduous leaves offset pine,
Ever so fine,
Beautiful blend
To comprehend.

Driving about soaking in the Fall colors along any roadside, the Sumac provide brilliant deep red. I loved the contrast with the green pines and other deciduous flora.

The use of the word peaking versus peeking was intentional.

This is a Minute poem.

The Minute Poem is a poem that follows the "8,4,4,4" syllable count structure. It usually has 3 stanzas that are exactly the same. So: 8,4,4,4; 8,4,4,4; 8,4,4,4 syllables.

A traditional Minute Poem has 12 lines total. It has 60 syllables (thus the Minute). It is written in a strict iambic meter. The rhyme scheme is as follows: aabb, ccdd, eeff.

Alliteration: roadside reds, beautiful blend, you'll yellow.

Assonance: the AU sound in "On Autumn", the O sound in "bound to collide" and "somewhere outside" as well as "spot touch yellow".

Consonance: of the L sound in "you'll yellow", the R sound in "color spreads".

Caesura: line 1.

This photograph was taken by the author in September 2011.

Poem #8:

THESE TREES
(A Whitney)

When some trees
The likes of these
Show colors
That really please
Orange and gold
Never gets old
To see blowing in the breeze

Color blooms on local Maple trees. Old Mansions make the backdrop for these mature trees near the Cathedral of St. Paul, Minnesota.

This poem is a Whitney.

A Whitney has a fixed syllable count of 3/4/3/4/3/4/7 in 7 lines.

Whitney Created by Betty Ann Whitney. This is a seven-line versed poem based on Japanese patterns that key off of syllable counts. The short, expressive lines carry a lively verse that resonates well to almost any subject.

No rhyme scheme is required, but may be incorporated if desired.

I added one of:

Aabacca.

Alliteration: blowing breeze.

Assonance: the EA sound in "really please", the O sound in "show colors" and "orange and gold", the E sound in "never gets".

Consonance: the L sound in "really please".

The picture was taken by the author along Summit Avenue in St. Paul, Minnesota.

Poem #9:

THEY FALL WHERE THEY MAY
(Sestet)

Autumn leaves fall wherever they may.
Trickling down all the day, I say.
Gathering on a cold ground
Anywhere they may be found.
These purple Maple leafs sublime
Have come to rest in this pretty pine.

Just a Fall thought.

This is a photograph of Maple leaves caught in the bough of a pine tree. It was taken in early October 2012, on Selby Avenue in St. Paul, Mn.

This poem is a sestet. A septet is a poem with six lines. In this one, I chose to vary the syllable count to provide a pleasing structure.

Syllable count 9,8,7,7,8,9.

Rhyme Scheme aabbcc.

Note here, that in the last two lines, I used near rhyme rather than perfect rhyme with the words sublime and pine.

I used in-line rhyme twice here:

Day, I say

They may

Alliteration: gathering ground, pretty pine.

Poem #10:

YELLOW LEAVES
(Whitney)

Autumn's touch
On old stone steps
Means fall's clutch
Is close at hand.
Yellow leaves
Color the land,
A time that we love so much

Old stone path with autumn leaves that have fallen across the path. I really liked the mix of pine and birch with the stone. Inspired this Whitney Poem.

A Whitney has a fixed syllable count of 3/4/3/4/3/4/7 in 7 lines. There is no required rhyme scheme, but I added one of: abacdca

Alliteration: on old, stone steps.

Assonance: of the O sound in "on old stone", and "love so". The A sound "at hand".

Consonance: the T sound in "autumn's touch", the L sound in "yellow leaves" and "color the land", the S sound in "is close".

This picture was taken by the author in an alley by the Cathedral of St. Paul.

CHAPTER 2: BIRDS

Birds are magnificent in their varying size, color of plumage, diversity of habits and habitats. Creatures of the air, trees, grasses and waters that never cease to fascinate. Great subjects for the poet's muse and the photographer's eye. Whether at the feeder, or in the air, they brighten our days with action and sound. They may delight us or awe us. Still or in motion, they are wonderful creatures that grace our lives.

Poem #11:

ANCIENT INSTINCTS

(A 5-7-5-7-7 Poem)

As leaves change colors,
Bird's thoughts carry far away.
Ancient instinct pulls.
Asking, is today the day?
Is it time to go or stay?

Don't you just wonder what this bird is thinking, sitting there on the autumn leaves? I did. This is what came to me.

This poem is a 5-7-5-7-7 Poem, not a Tanka.

A Tanka poem must follow all the rules of Japanese poetry, while a 5-7-5-7-7 poem does not. For example, Tanka consist of five units (often treated as separate lines when romanized or translated) usually with the following pattern of: 5-7-5-7-7.

The 5-7-5 is called the kami-no-ku "upper phrase", and the 7-7 is called the shimo-no-ku "lower phrase".

Traditionally tanka has had no concept of rhyme Indeed, certain arrangements of rhymes, even accidental, were considered dire faults in a poem. Also, Japanese poems do not have capitalization or punctuation. They also have strict rules on how to format the poem's title. So, that is why this poem is definitely not a Tanka.

Alliteration: change colors.

Assonance: the A sounds in "carry far away", the I sound in "is it", the O sounds in "to go or".

Consonance: the R sound in "carry far", the T sound in "ancient instinct" and "it time".

In-line Rhyme: today the day.

Caesura: line 4.

Poem #12:

BALTIMORE ORIOLES
(A Lisalet Poem)

Saw a bright flash of orange across the sky,
Startled by such rich color and a song.
Sitting twixt the twigs, raising spirits high,
Not just one, but two birds had come along.

Startled by such rich color and a song,
I stood transfixed, afraid that they would fly.
Before they left, they fluted sweet and long.
Saw a bright flash of orange across the sky.

Sitting twixt the twigs, raising spirits high,
To get too close and scare them would be wrong.
Stood there frozen, not wanting a goodbye,
Startled by such rich color and a song.

Not just one, but two birds had come along.
Beauty of Orioles, you can't deny.
Their colorful countenances do belong
Sitting twixt the twigs, raising spirits high.

I was out walking today and spotted these two birds. I was so excited that I was able to get my lens on them.

This is a Lisalet Poem, a style created by Lisa Sherman on FanStory, that has a fixed format of repeating lines, and when rhymed, a forced set of only two rhyme choices in an abab rhyme scheme.

The format repeats the first four lines in a structured reverse cascade down the stanzas as follows:

1/2/3/4 2/5/6/1 3/7/8/2 4/9/10/3,

such that the stanzas incorporate the repeating lines as 1/2 2/1 3/2 4/3 for the first and last lines of each stanza.

The optional rhyme scheme becomes ABCD BabA CbcB DcdC, although C and D also rhyme with AB, and the capitals represent the repeated lines. I hope that all makes sense.

I chose the syllable count to be 10, but that is not a requirement.

Alliteration: startled such song, twixt twigs, that they, would wrong, colorful countenances.

Assonance: the O sound in "of orange across", the O sound in "stood goodbye" and "of Orioles" and "do belong".

Consonance: the TW sound in "twixt twigs", the L sound in "left fluted long", the N sound in "not wanting".

Caesura: Line 4, Line 6, line 7, line 9, line 11, line 13, line 14 and line 16.

The photograph is from my personal collection. Took May 14, 2013.

Poem #13:

CHICKADEE
(A Tic Tac Toe Poem)

Chickadee, | *likes to flit,* | *endlessly*
_____

Hops about, | *in a tree,* | *sounding out*
_____

Voice set free, | *Sweet notes hit,* | *melody*

If you ever watched a Chickadee you'll notice that they don't sit still very long. They flit from branch to branch, then swoop down to grab their food, then take off to eat it in the tree. Then they'll sing and chirp. I tried to capture that here.

Just doing some style experimentation here. I created this format after playing Tic Tac Toe with my grandson. The idea is to have a poem that, in segments, can be read across, down, or down diagonally in any direction. This poem has 3 lines of 9 syllables, with every third syllable a rhyme (a segment). The first rhyme crisscrosses into an X. The Poem ends up in a square pattern like Tic-Tac-Toe. Here is the required rhyme pattern in the square. See how the A's cross.

A B A
C A C
A B A

Alliteration: set sweet.

Assonance: the O sound in "hops about" and "sounding out", the E sounds in "set free sweet".

Consonance: the L sound in "likes flit endlessly".

In-line Rhyme: Chickadee endlessly, about out, free melody.

The Photograph is mine of a Chickadee flitting off with its food.

Poem #14:

COMES THE MUSE
(Anaphoric with Refrain)

When I see a baby cry,
When I have a teary eye,
When I ask the Question - Why?
When I want to say -Goodbye,
Comes the Muse.

When I watch a garden grow,
When a mountain's topped with snow,
When I see the waters flow,
When I feel the moonlight's glow,
Comes the Muse.

When the secrets all unfold,
When I need the story told,
When my thoughts are getting bold,
When a love is getting old,
Comes the Muse.

'Tis the spark that lights the fire,
'Tis the point that drives desire,
'Tis the burning, churning pyre,
'Tis the raging, rasping, ire,
'Tis the Muse!

'Tis the pain within my soul,
'Tis the grasping, pulling whole,
'Tis the hot and searing coal,
'Tis the masterswitch control,
'Tis the Muse!

'Tis high hint of creativity,
'Tis the words that want to be,
'Tis in everything I see,
'Tis my spirit breaking free,
'Tis my Muse!

This is how I describe that moment when I get inspired. Almost anything can set it off, but when it happens, it freely flies.

This poem is Anaphoric.

Often used in political speeches and occasionally in prose and poetry, anaphora is the repetition of a word or words at the beginning of successive phrases, clauses, or lines to create a verbal reinforcing effect. I like how it powerfully drives the stanzas.

I also used mono-rhyme in each stanza.

Alliteration: garden grow, drives desire, raging rasping, high hint, words want,

Assonance: the Y sound in "baby cry", the E sound in "teary eye", the O sounds in "mountains topped" and "moonlight's glow" as well as "story told", the I sounds in "pain within".

Consonance: the T sound in "thoughts getting", the P sound in "grasping pulling", the S sound in "master switch".

In-line rhyme: burning churning

Anaphora: the when's, the 'Tis', and the "Comes the Muse".

Caesura:line 3, line 4, line 18, line 19, and line 21.

This photograph that I took on a blue cold February morning of two Canadian Geese, exploding from the surface of a frozen pond in perfect tandem, most closely represents the essence of the Muse as my thoughts fly free.

Poem #15:

THE COOT'S CALL
(Triolet - 3)

In tall swamp grass a Coot did hide,
Near fallen timber by the side.
Through shallow water saw it glide
In tall swamp grass a Coot did hide,
With plaintive duck calling, it cried,
A plea that carried on the tide.
In tall swamp grass a Coot did hide,
Near fallen timber by the side.

I saw the pearly white duck bill,
In tall swamp grass a Coot did hide,
Was barely noticed from the hill.
I saw the pearly white duck bill.
To spot it gave us all a thrill,
We took the whole swamp sight in stride.
I saw the pearly white duck bill,
In tall swamp grass a Coot did hide.

In tall swamp grass a Coot did hide,
So lonely, looking for a mate.
It searched the site, both far and wide,
In tall swamp grass a Coot did hide.
It wanted cute Coot duck for bride.
The chance is great; he'll find love's fate.
In tall swamp grass a Coot did hide,
So lonely, looking for a mate.

The American Coot Duck is distinguishable by its white bill and dark gray/black body. I thought it was a log, until I heard it cry out. They are small ducks that are usually in a sizeable group, but this one was solitary. Thus the genesis of the poem.

This poem is a suite of 3 linked Triolets. A Triolet is a poem of only eight lines with a rhyme scheme ABaAabAB. The fourth and seventh lines are the same exact line as the first. The eighth line is the same exact line as the second.

I wrote this one in iambic tetrameter, and did a bit of inversion in the middle on the rhyme. The first stanza is also mono-rhymed which is somewhat of a departure.

Alliteration: swamp sight stride, lonely looking, searched site, cute Coot, find fate.

Assonance: the A sound in "tall swamp grass a", the I sound in "did hide" and "it glide", the E sound in "plea carried".

Consonance: the W sound in "shallow water saw", the C sound in "duck calling it cried",

the T sound in "to spot it", the L sound in "all a thrill", the W sound in "whole swamp".

In-line Rhyme: great fate.

Caesura: line 5, line 18, line 19, line 22, line 24.

The photograph was taken by the author during his camping trip over Memorial Day Weekend, 2013.

Poem #16:

GOLDFINCHES FEEDING
(A Rondel Poem)

Three golden birds with golden song
Flew in to eat sunflower seed.
Bright feathers flashing color creed
Of deepest hue to come along.

I hope they feel that they belong
In my backyard. I'll feed their need.
Three golden birds with golden song
Flew in to eat sunflower seed.

As my delight has risen strong,
This joy, I hope time won't impede
As feathers frolic, Finches feed.
I pray their stay I might prolong
Three golden birds with golden song.

Beautiful Goldfinches eating sunflower seeds.

This poem is a Rondel. A Rondel is a verse form originating in French lyrical poetry, later used in the verse of other languages as well, such as English and Romanian. It is a variation of the Rondeau consisting of two quatrains followed by a quintet (13 lines total) or a sestet (14 lines total). The Rondel was created in the 14th century.

It is a poem of fixed format with repeating lines and structured number of lines per stanza. The first and second lines repeat in the middle of the poem and at the end. Although, only the first line repeats at the end. There is an option to repeat both.

The rhyme scheme is normally ABba abAB abbaA(B), where the capital letters shown here are the repeated lines and the parenthesis shows the possible option.

There is no specific meter or syllable count in this style, but 8 is the most commonly used. For this poem, I chose to use a fixed count of 8 in iambic tetrameter.

Alliteration: sunflower seed, feathers flashing, color creed, that they, feathers frolic Finches feed, pray prolong.

Assonance: the E sound in "deepest hue", the O sound in "to come along".

Consonance: the T sound in "to eat" and "bright feathers", the S sound in "has risen", and the T sound in "time won't".

Caesura: line 6, line 10, line 11.

In-line Rhyme: feed need, pray stay.

Actually, this photograph was not taken in my backyard, but rather at the Minnesota National Wildlife Refuge near the airport in Bloomington, Minnesota, in April of 2012.

Poem #17:

HE SPREADS HIS WINGS
(Modified Octogram)

A Mallard lifts from lake to sky
He spreads his wings
To reach aloft and freely fly.
He skyward springs
As feathers flare, his wings swing wide,
Displays the grays on underside,
When feathered physics get applied,
He spreads his wings.

This bird has character galore
That color brings.
Fluorescent shades, the basic core
'Round head it rings,
As sunshine turns it blue or green,
It changes with a splendid sheen,
Amazing sight, you've ever seen,
He spreads his wings.

A Mallard duck can lift off water nearly vertically. Depending on the angle of the sun, the male's head and neck, which has fluorescent feathers, appears either green, or blue.

I modified an Octogram for this poem.

The Octogram is a style of poetry invented by Fanstorian Sally Yocom (S. Yocom). It consists of two stanzas of eight lines each, with a very specific syllable count and rhyme scheme.

Syllable count is 84848884, repeat on second stanza.

Rhyme scheme: ABabccbB ababddbB, where B repeats same text.

For this poem I changed it to ABabcccB ababdddB to create a three line rhyme on the triple eights.

No more than 16 lines.

The tempo is tetrameter on the 8 count line, and dimeter on the 4 count line, but not iambic.

Alliteration: lifts lake, freely fly, skyward springs, feathers flare, wings wide, round rings, splendid sheen, and sight seen.

Assonance: the A sound in "character galore", the U sound in "turns blue".

Consonance: the K sound in "lake sky", the L sound in "aloft freely fly", the W sound in "wings swing wide", the N sound in "on underside", the F sound in "feathered physics", the S sound in "fluorescent shades basic", the C sound in "basic core", the V sound in "you've ever".

Caesura: line 5, line 11, line 15.

In-line Rhyme: wings swing, displays grays.

The photograph was taken by the author at Battle Creek Park of Maplewood, Minnesota, in March 2013.

Poem #18:

RUDDY DUCK
(ABAB Quatrain)

I just saw a Ruddy Duck
It was sitting in the pond
I couldn't believe my luck
Rare species of which I'm fond

This is a Ruddy Duck. Known for its ruddy brown body and blue bill.

This poem is written as an abab rhyming Quatrain. It has a meter with 7 syllables.

Limited punctuation intended by the author.

Alliteration: none

Assonance: the U sounds in "just ruddy duck", the I sound in "it sitting in".

Consonance: the D sounds in "ruddy duck", the T sounds in "it sitting".

Took this photograph April 28, 2013, at Minomini Park in Woodbury, Minnesota.

Poem #19:

SIZE SURPRISE
(Tanka)

very large blue bird
curiously seeks a meal
taken aback when
small red-winged blackbird attacks
fierce when the family's at risk

Red-winged Blackbird attacks a stunned Great Blue Heron

This poem is a Japanese form of poetry known as a Tanka.

A Tanka is another poetry type related to the haiku. The first three lines are unrhymed. They have a syllable count of five, seven, five, like the haiku. But the last two lines both have seven syllables. So the syllable count is: (5, 7, 5, 7, 7).

Alliteration: blue bird, fierce family.

Assonance: the A sound in "taken aback", the E sound in "seeks meal".

Consonance: the K sound in "taken aback", the L sound in "large blue", the CK sounds in "blackbirds attacks".

Author's photograph taken at a pond behind Treasure Island Casino near Red Wing, Minnesota.

Poem #20:

TWO MATED DUCKS

(Rondeau)

Two mated ducks swim into sunset's glow,
On golden pond, where ripples clearly show
The path from whence these two did take their start,
To drift into this peaceful work of art,
Creating such contentment as they go.

No wind upon this silent scene did blow,
To mar the mirror, as the waters flow.
With sun's reflection, as twilights depart,
Two mated ducks.

Then silhouettes shade shore as shadows grow,
The ducks, two darkened shapes lined in a row,
They make a master's image on my heart.
This moment makes it hard for me to part!
Yet, what a perfect privilege to know
Two mated ducks.

Two ducks in silhouette on a Lake at Sunset.

This Poem is a Rondeau.

A Rondeau is a fixed form of poetry. It is often used in light or witty poems. It often has fifteen octo - or decasyllabic lines with three stanzas. It usually only has two rhymes used in the poem. A word or words from the first part of the first line are used as a refrain ending the second and third stanzas.

The rhyme scheme is

aabba aabR aabbaR, where the R represents the repeated refrain.

I used a syllabic count of 10 for this poem.

Alliteration: swim sunset's, creating contentment, silent scene, mar mirror,

silhouettes shade shore as shadows, ducks darkened, make master's , moment makes, perfect privilege.

Assonance: the O sound in "on golden pond show", the I sound in "drift into this" and "lined in".

Consonance: the R sound in "where ripples", the W sound in "whence two", the T sound in "two take their start", the M sound in make master's image my", and the T sound in "Yet what".

Caesura: line 2, line 7, line 8, line 11, line 14.

This photograph was taken by the author at Lake Phalen, in St. Paul, Mn.

Poem #21:

WARM EARTH
(5-7-5 Poem)

warm Earth wakes the worm
basks in the glow of spring sun
robin gets its meal

Robins return, worms beware, a typical spring scenario.

This poem is a 5-7-5 Poem.

A 5-7-5 follows the structure of a Haiku. It has three lines. The first line has 5 syllables. The second line has 7 syllables. The third line has 5 syllables again.

While a Senryu, is primarily concerned with human nature. A Haiku, primarily concerned with physical nature. A 5-7-5 poem is a free form with the only limitation being the syllable count. It could be about anything, from food to writing, feelings to phobias.

Alliteration: warm wakes worm, spring sun

Assonance: the O sound in "glow of".

Consonance: the TS sound in "gets its".

The photograph is from author's collection.

Poem #22:

WOOD DUCKS
(A Triolet Poem)

When wood ducks float on by,
They sail with painted grace.
They really catch the eye,
When wood ducks float on by.
Especially when you spy
Male's decorated face.
When wood ducks float on by,
They sail with painted grace.

A pair of Wood Ducks, male and female. Known by the male's colorful head crest and defining white outlines. The female looks quite drab beside him.

This poem is a Triolet

A Triolet is a poem with a fixed format. This one has a syllable structure of 8 counts (or tetrameter). It is a poem of only eight lines with a rhyme scheme of only two rhymes (a and b) that can be represented as follows:

ABaAabAB,

where the fourth and seventh lines are the same exact line as the first. The eighth line is the same exact line as the second (This is represented by the capital letters shown).

Thus, it is very important to compose the first two lines carefully so that the entire poem flows well and is enhanced by the repeats.

Alliteration: when wood.

Assonance: the O sounds in "wood float on", the A sound in "sail painted grace" and "decorated face".

Consonance: the T sound in "with painted", the SP sounds in "especially spy".

This is a picture taken by the author in May, 2013.

CHAPTER 3: FLOWERS

For overall beauty, it is hard to beat the flower. Such variety of size, shape and color is a poet's, as well as photographer's dream. Some have been beautifully cultured and domesticated. Others are wildflowers. There's even the lowly weed. All of them are unique and exquisite. This chapter gives the reader a sampling of each.

Poem #23:

ALFALFA

(An Octogram)

Alfalfa blooms with bursting buds,
Purple and white.
Not the stuff of songs and ballads,
They still excite.
It's often confused with clover.
If you closely look it over,
You'll enjoy a delightful sight,
Purple and white.

Frequently used farming methods:
Setting soil right,
Fine hay for horse feed and cow cuds,
They chew and bite.
Makes it a healthy forage food!
Their flowers set a lovely mood.
Alfalfa blooms with bursting buds,
Purple and white.

Another flower in my wildflower series.

Alfalfa is one of the oldest cultivated crops, but wild seeds have escaped and grown freely across the country side. Thought to have originated in ancient Iran, it is also known as Lucerne. Its classification is Medicago sativa, named in the fourth century AD by Roman writer Palladius. The Medica handle came from the fact that a people called the Medes, lived in that region of Iran at the time. Today, it is used as the most nutritious hay to feed horses and cows. It is also used to balance soils through crop rotation.

This poem is an Octogram.

The Octogram is a style of poetry invented by Fanstorian Sally Yocom (S.Yocom). It consists of two stanzas of eight lines each, with a very specific syllable count and rhyme scheme.

Syllable count is:

84848884, repeat on second stanza.

Rhyme scheme:

ABabccbB ababddbB, where B repeats same text.

For this poem I changed it to:

ABabccbB ababddAB.

No more than 16 lines.

The tempo is tetrameter on the 8 count line, and dimeter on the 4 count line, but not iambic.

Alliteration: blooms bursting buds, stuff songs, confused clover, frequently farming, setting soil, hay horse, cow cuds, forage food.

Assonance: the O sound in "of songs" and in "often confused clover" and "closely look over", the OR sound in "for horse".

Consonance: the T sounds in "still excite", the L sound in "you'll delightful".

I took this photograph on June 23, 2013, while on a walk in the park with my wife.

Poem #24:

CAROLINA ROSE
(A Triolet)

This wild red rose brings bold beauty
To the hedges and open fields.
She's a Carolina cutey.
This wild red rose brings bold beauty,
A pure prickly southern gypsy.
So beware of the spikes she wields.
This wild red rose brings bold beauty
To the hedges and open fields.

This Rose is a wildflower known as the Carolina Rose (Rosa Carolina) that is fairly common across most parts of the US and Canada, from the Mississippi eastward. It can be found in white, pink, or red along road sides, hedges, fields, and prairies. In fact, it also known as the Pasture Rose. It can be distinguished from other wild roses by its very thin straight spikes along its stem. Other roses have thicker curved spikes.

This is part of my wildflower series.

There is also a popular Bluegrass singer named Carolina Rose, who took her name from this flower and her own Southern heritage.

This poem is a Triolet.

A Triolet is a poem with a fixed format. This one has a syllable structure of 8 counts or tetrameter. It is a poem of only eight lines with a rhyme scheme of only two rhymes (a and b) that can be represented as follows: ABaAabAB,

where the fourth and seventh lines are the same exact line as the first. The eighth line is the same exact line as the second (This is represented by the capital letters shown). Thus, it is very important to compose the first two lines carefully so that the entire poem flows well and is enhanced by the repeats.

Alliteration: red rose, brings bold beauty, Carolina cutie, pure prickly, so spikes she,

Assonance: the E sounds in "the hedges open fields", the A sound in "a Carolina".

Consonance: the P sounds in "pure prickly gypsy, the W sound in "beware wields"

This photograph was taken by the author himself, while on a walk in July, 2012.

Poem #25:

CINQUEFOIL, FIVE HEARTS
(ABCB Quatrains)

Tiny little Cinquefoil,
When viewed from up above,
Only has five petals,
But each one speaks of love.

It's quite a little beauty
In its color and shape.
This flower's a cutie.
They're beauty can't escape.

So while you're out walking
And spot five tiny hearts,
That may get you gawking,
Heed the message they impart.

That, Love is Everywhere!
Don't be afraid to share.

This wildflower is Sulfur Cinquefoil. It is a very little beauty that is such a small, unobtrusive flower, that you might walk right past it, and not notice it. That would be sad, because these are very expressive little ones. The name Cinquefoil comes from "cingue", meaning five, and "foil", meaning leaves or petals. Indeed these have 5 petals. But look! Each is a tiny little heart. As such, they have been revered for ages. They can be found in medieval heraldry meaning strength, power, honor, and loyalty. Also known in Europe as Potentilla, they are frequently called "Barren Strawberries". According to Wikipedia, this five petaled flower was used in the architecture of numerous churches in Normandy and Brittany, through the 15th century. As early as 1033, it showed up in the church at Ruellie-Vergy, Burgandy, France. It was worn on the coat of arms of Bardolph of Bretagne. Medicinally, they have been used to treat diarrhea.

So, as you are out and about, stop and look at the tiny wildflowers that grow alongside the path.

This poem is a set of 3 quatrains followed by a pair of rhyming couplets. The rhyme scheme is a simple abcb. The syllable count is 6.

Alliteration: while walking, get gawking.

Assonance: the I sounds in "tiny little cinquefoil" and in "it's quite little" and "in its" as well as "fine tiny", the E sound in "when viewed" and "heed message they", the O sound in "one of love" and "so you're out", the A sound in "and shape", the A sound in that "may gawking", the EA sound in "each speaks".

Consonance: the L sound in "only petals", the T sound in "quite little beauty" and "that get", the C sounds in "can't escape", the L sound in "while walking",

This picture was taken in a park in Maplewood, Minnesota, on June 11, 2013, by the author.

Poem #26:

DAISIES IN THE DAYLIGHT

(A Triolet Poem)

Daylight shining on the daisy,
Fills darkened days with bright delight.
When the world is looking hazy,
Daylight shining on the daisy,
Brings peace to what's looking crazy,
Compared to beauty that's so bright.
Daylight shining on the daisy,
Fills darkened days with bright delight.

I went for a walk and found these lovely wild daisies that inspired this poem.

This poem is a Triolet.

A Triolet poem is an 8 line poem with a fixed format and repeating lines. Line one and two get repeated. Line one repeated on line four and seven. Line two repeats on line eight only. There is also a fixed rhyme scheme of only two rhymes. The scheme is:

ABaAabAB, where the capital letters represent the repeated lines.

Alliteration: bright delight, darkened days, when world, beauty bright.

Assonance: the O sound in "world looking".

Consonance: the L sound in "fills delight", the R sound in "brings crazy".

In-line rhyme: bright delight.

This picture was taken by the author on June 25, 2013.

Poem #27:

FLUTED PETALS
(A 5-7-5 Poem)

yellow tinged maroon
bright fluted flower petals
surrealistic

Unknown flower, but some think that it is a dahlia. At any rate, those petals are very unique. They look like little trumpets, or each a separate lily.

This poem is a 5-7-5 Poem.

A 5-7-5 follows the structure of a Haiku. It has three lines. The first line has 5 syllables. The second line has 7 syllables. The third line has 5 syllables again.

While a Senryu, is primarily concerned with human nature. A Haiku, primarily concerned with physical nature. A 5-7-5 poem is a free form with the only limitation being the syllable count. It could be about anything, from food to writing, feelings to phobias.

Alliteration: fluted flower.

Consonance: the T and L sounds in "Fluted flower petals".

Author's photograph.

Poem #28:

HANGING FLOWERS
(A Dizain Poem)

This pretty hanging flower pot
Adds beauty to the walking trail,
Near river where we walk a lot.
Such brilliant color hues prevail,
In red, gold, blue, and pink detail.

Held suspended on metal chains,
To catch the drops of summer rains,
Bright blooms spill out to float on air.
An awesome bud array remains,
Delighting people walking there.

I was out walking along the Mississippi River one afternoon with my wife and grandson. The winding walkway has these hanging flower pots on posts every 10 yards or so. I am teaching photography to my 9 year old grandson. So, I asked him to take a picture of one. This is it.

This poem is a Dizain. I was introduced to this format when I reviewed a poem by FanStorian, Honeycomb, called "I'm Not Alone". Her's was a lovely spiritual poem.

A Dizain is a ten line poem with either 8 or 10 syllables. I have used eight.

The rhyme scheme is:

ababb ccdcd

In a Dizian you can divide the poem, if you wish, into two five line stanzas, or two four line stanzas and a couplet. I chose the first format.

So the first stanza ends with a rhyming couplet after alternating rhymed lines. While the second stanza starts with one. Sort of reverse mirrored rhymes.

Alliteration: to the trail, where we walk, bright bloom, an awesome array.

Assonance: The Os in "flower pot", the ER sound in "near where", and the O sound in "drops of" and "blooms out to float on", and the A sound in "array remains".

Consonance: the R in "near river where", the Ls in "brilliant color prevails", the T sounds in "to catch the".

Caerura: line 5.

This picture is part of the author's personal collection.

Poem #29:

SILKEN SWIRLS
(A Canzone Poem)

What beauty bursts in silken swirls from the rose.
Rich the hues this bush imbues,
Inspiring bards of yore to exalting prose,
While fragrance delights the nose.

Such treasures locked within nature's tiny gift,
Helping sagging spirits lift,
As shades of red set artistic minds adrift,
Aromatic airs are sniffed.

Who can conceive such things as this!
Perfection held in flowered bliss!

I went to the Rose Garden located at Lake Harriet in Minneapolis. It has a stunning display of roses that were in full bloom. The garden has several flower beds and two fountains. It is outdoors and open, free to the public. This is just one example of the beauties that you'll find there.

This poem is a Canzone.

CANZONE: An Italian lyric poem of varying stanza length, usually written in a mixture of hendecasyllables (11) and heptasyllables (7) with a concluding short stanza or envoi. May be abab or aabb. This is a very short one.

Alliteration: beauty bursts, silken swirls, treasures tiny, sagging spirits, shades set , artistic adrift, aromatic airs are, can conceive.

Assonance: the Os in "from rose", the U sounds in "hues bush imbues", the O sound in "of yore to", the I sounds in "within tiny gift" and "spirits lift", the AIR sound in "aromatic airs". Finally, the E sounds in "perfection held".

Consonance: the T sounds in "set artistic adrift", the D sound in "shades red", the S sound in "as shades" and in "such things as this".

In-line Rhyme: hues imbues.

This photograph was taken by the author himself at the Lake Harriet Rose Garden.

CHAPTER 4: INSECTS

Insects can be beautiful, as the butterfly; strange, like the spider or scorpion; or ugly, like the stink bug. You wouldn't think there's much to be poetic about in this group, but maybe that's not true. The author hopes this chapter will give a better appreciation for the topic and the creatures that are its subject matter.

Poem #30:

BRITTLE WINGS
(A Whitney Poem with 5-7-5)

Brittle wings
Past battles won
Beauty sings
Grace in the sun
To survive
Bad blows are done
Still gloriously alive

Brittle wings in sky
Battered Buckeye Butterfly
I Watched you fly by

I had a picture of this Buckeye butterfly with battered wings. It got me to write this Poem. I was inspired by a poem that I reviewed this morning written by cheyennewy, a fellow FanStorian, called Frayed Edges. It reminded me that I had this picture.

There are two poem styles here, a Whitney followed by a 5-7-5 Poem.

A Whitney has a fixed syllable count of 3/4/3/4/3/4/7 in 7 lines.

The rhyme scheme is : ababcbc

The other format is obvious. The 5-7-5 is mono-rhymed.

Alliteration: bad blows, battered Buckeye Butterfly.

Assonance: the I sound in "brittle wings", the A sound in "past battles", the O sound in "blows done".

Consonance: the N sound in "in sun", and all the L sounds in "Still gloriously alive".

In-line Rhyme: fly by.

This picture by taken by the author in June, 2012, in a little park in Cottage Grove, Minnesota.

Poem #31:

BUTTERFLY ON JOE PYE
(An Octelle Poem)

Pretty mops for healer Joe Pye
Power from food of butterfly
Nectar is sweet on the vine
For fevers it's very fine
Find them near pond any day
Pink tops you spot far away
Pretty mops for healer Joe Pye
Power from food of butterfly

A Monarch butterfly on Joe Pye Weed.

Joe Pye Weed is actually an amazing wildflower that is an herb, a butterfly plant, and an ornamental bush. It is usually found in the wild near wetlands and ponds. It grows in a thick cluster that provides excellent cover for birds, butterflies, insects, and small mammals. Its scientific name is Eupatorium Purpureum, which is a member of the Aster family. Distinguishable as a large plant with purple or pink mops of tiny tuberous flowers, it is easily spotted. It is also called, Queen of the Field. It is named after a legendary healer named Joe Pye or Jopi, a New England Indian who helped cure early colonists of fevers and Typhus using this herb. Native Americans may also have used it for kidney stones and urinary tract infections.

This poem is an Octelle. The Octelle has eight lines. It uses personification and symbolism in a telling manner.

-The syllable count is 8, 8, 7, 7, 7, 7, 8, 8.

-The rhyme scheme is aa - bb - cc - aa.

-The first two lines and the last two lines are identical.

Alliteration: from food, for fevers fine.

Assonance: The Os in "Power from food of", the V sound in "fevers very", The A sound in "any day" and "far away".

Consonance: the P sounds in "tops spot" and "pretty mops", the N sounds in "find near pond any".

Mirror word use: "Tops" spelled backwards is "spot".

This photograph was taken by the author along the Mississippi River on August 3, 2013.

Poem #32:

DRAGONFLY, SETTLE BY

(A Shadorma Poem)

Dragonfly,
With fast flights so bold,
Settle by.
Show off why,
Your agile wings fill the sky,
Body black and gold.

Such big eyes,
How you view the world.
My surprise!
Off he flies,
When sudden wind lift applies,
See-through wings unfurl.

A Widow Skimmer Dragonfly alights on a stick in a field near my house. Agile aerial acrobats that whisk and hover about. They can fly at great speeds. It's hard to get a picture of one. This one settled down a bit.

This poem is a Shadorma, actually two. A Shardoma is a short poem of six lines (a sestet) with a fixed syllable count of 3/5/3/3/7/5. This gives it a lively, expressive tempo. It can either be free verse or rhymed.

I chose to rhyme it. I used abaaab.

Alliteration: fast flight, body black, when wind.

Assonance: the O sound in "so bold" and "show off" and also "body gold".

Consonance: the W sound in sound in "show why" and "how view world", the G sound in "agile wings", the F sound in "off flies", the L sound in "lift applies".

In-line Rhyme: you view.

This picture was actually taken by my grandson, JT, when I let him try my Kodak 981 digital camera.

Poem #33:

PEARLY-EYE BUTTERFLY

(Quintet with refrains)

Pearly-eye butterfly alights.
Its jeweled wings spread such delights!
Beguiling in brown-tinted hues,
The delicacy it imbues
Can drive away the deepest blues -

When it alights.

It sits there on a fragile twig
That really isn't very big,
Amongst the branches of a tree
Poised there, posed so regally.
I stop to watch it quietly -

When it alights.

I pondered where this creature's been;
How far and long it's travelin'.
I really wouldn't be surprised
At wonders seen with all those eyes.
Believe a shaded rest applies -

When it alights.

This is a Pearly-Eye Butterfly (Enodia Anthedon). Known for the spots on its wings that are like little pearls. The wings have a brown tint with a touch of purple. This butterfly is unique in that it likes shade, it isn't attracted to flowers, and it flies later in the day than most other butterflies (often as late as 8 PM). It is a North American species that has a range from central Saskatchewan and Nebraska across Canada to Nova Scotia, then south as low as Alabama and Mississippi. There is usually one generation per year. They travel far and wide, then seek the shade to rest and mate. They like tree sap from willows, birch, and poplars. The light green caterpillars feed on grasses. Those born late in the season hibernate over the winter. Source: Wikipedia.

This poem is written with 5 lined stanzas (Quintets) and a repeating refrain after each. The rhyme scheme is aabbb. The syllable count is 8.

Alliteration: spread such, beguiling brown-tinted, drive deepest, poised posed, wonders with it imbues.

Assonance: the I sound in "it alights", the O sounds in "poised posed so" and "stop to".

Consonance: the L sounds in "Pearly-eye Butterfly alights", the W in "jeweled wings", the G sound in "fragile twig", the R sounds in "pondered where creature's", the S sound in "those eyes".

Caesura: line 10.

In-line Rhyme: Pearly-eye Butterfly, it sits.

This picture is a photograph taken by the author himself at Lake Elmo Park Preserve in Minnesota on July 20, 2013.

Poem #34:

SITS IN SAND
(A Haiku)

Velvet Butterfly
regally sits lakeshore sand
filigreed wings ripple

A beautiful Mourning Cloak sits on the shore at Red Lake in Northern Minnesota. It has a lovely velvety coating on its wings, and a filigree lace at the bottom. I was excited to see and photograph it.

This poem is a Haiku, using an Americanized,

special Japanese format. A Haiku is a very short form typically characterized by three qualities:

1. The essence of haiku is "cutting" (kiru). This is often represented by the juxtaposition of two images or ideas and "cutting word" between them, a kind of verbal punctuation mark which signals the moment of separation and colors the manner in which the juxtaposed elements are related.

2. Traditional Haiku consists of three phrases of 5, 7 and 5, respectively. 17 syllables.

3. A seasonal reference, usually drawn from an extensive but defined list of such words.

It can also be written in less than 17 syllables. Commonly a 3, 5, and 3 pattern is used, but anything under 17 syllables is acceptable.

Some other aspects of a pure Japanese Haiku are:

No capitals (broke that rule).

No rhyming.

No alliteration (broke that rule in the title).

The formal format of a Haiku title is: haiku (title), there the title has no capital letters. (broke that rule).

Assonance: the I in "wings ripple".

Consonance: the G sound in "filigreed wings".

Picture taken by author September, 2012.

CHAPTER 5: PATHWAYS

As we journey through our lives we walk on many different paths. Some are crossroads. Some take us to the unknown. Others are familiar, well warn, and comforting. Whatever the case, they transition us from here - to there. Here in this chapter I describe a couple that I have found. Join me in this walk.

Poem #35:

ANGRY ANCIENT OAKS
(A Sonnet)

The ancient oaks that guard this glen
Are jealous of the folks who come.
For they suspect the "where" and "when",
Of stranger's past they're coming from.

As they've been fooled by cheats before,
Of forest treasures come to steal,
To strip the wood and leave the floor
So barren, it took years to heal.

So, let them know that you're a friend.
Despoil not any sacred ground!
Leave only footprints in the end.
All else, leave as it was first found.

Then angry looks will turn to smiles,
And nature will rejoice for miles.

I was walking in the forest, and came upon this glen of oak trees. They looked like they had angry faces and raised this poem out of me.

This poem is in sonnet format of 14 lines, three quatrains in abab rhyming and a closing rhymed couplet. Written in iambic tetrameter.

The photograph is one taken of this glen this weekend. Since the trees look alive to me, this poem will become part of my animated stills collection.

Alliteration: guard glen, where when, by before, first found, them that.

Assonance: the O sounds in "folks who come", the E sounds in "forest treasures steal", the O sound in "wood Floor" and "so know you're", the EA sound in "years heal".

Consonance: the Fs in "fore fooled before", the S sounds in "stranger's past", the L sound in "all else".

Caesura: line 8, line 9, line 12.

This picture was taken at the Lake Elmo Preserve on Memorial Day, 2013.

Poem #36:

FALL TRAIL
(A 5-7-5 Poem)

Colorful fall trail
winding in wonderful ways
leaves an impression

A favorite Autumn walkway.

This poem is a 5-7-5 formatted poem, an American version of the Japanese Haiku, only without all the formal requirements of a Haiku.

As such it contains only 3 lines designated by their syllable count.

Line 1: 5 syllables.

Line 2: 7 syllables.

Line 3: 5 syllables.

Alliteration: winding wonderful ways.

Consonance: the L sounds in "colorful fall trail".

This photograph was taken by the author himself at a local park in Maplewood, Minnesota.

Poem #37:

IVY ARCHWAY
(Modified Triolet)

The proper path was clearly marked
In ivy dressed on solid stone.
To destination you embarked,
The proper path was clearly marked.
Imposing when the way is arched,
And where the lovely vines have grown.
In ivy dressed on solid stone,
The proper path was clearly marked.

"Follow the walk to the Ivy Archway"

When the path is this clear, it is easy to identify.

This poem is a modified Triolet.

A Triolet is a poem of only eight lines with a rhyme scheme of:

ABaAabAB.

The fourth and seventh lines are the same exact line as the first. The eighth line is the same exact line as the second.

However, this one is modified because I reversed the last two repeat lines. So the rhyme scheme is:

ABaAabBA

The meter is iambic tetrameter.

Alliteration: proper path, in ivy, solid stone, when way.

Assonance: the O sounds in "on solid stone", the O sound in "to you".

Consonance: the R sound in "clearly marked", the V sound in "lovely vines".

This photograph was taken by the author, down near the Cathedral of St. Paul, Minnesota, in October, 2012.

Poem #38:

LIGHT AT THE END

(Septets)

In the deepest, darkest hour,
When you've given up all hope,
While you're trembling and you cower,
At the ending of your rope,
Your confidence soon will flower,
And you'll learn that you can cope,
When light shines at the end of the tunnel.

As you stumble in the darkness,
And you think you've lost your way,
In the labyrinth of starkness,
On October's blackest day,
Do you think you'll find your mark? Yes!
I am confident you'll say,
When light shines at the end of the tunnel.

When you think your dreams are shattered,
And are buried in the ground,
You've lost everything that mattered,
And there's no hope to be found,
Well, those fears will all be scattered,
And your faith will soon rebound,
When light shines at the end of the tunnel.

There is always hope.

Why October? That's the month when the dead rise on All Soul's Day, Halloween.

This poem is a Septet.

A septet is simply a poem with 7 lines of any style, format, or meter.

For this I chose an anapestic meter of seven syllables.

The rhyme scheme is:

abababR,

where the R is the repeated refrain.

Alliteration: deepest darkest, you're you, on October's, can cope.

Assonance: the O sound in "of your rope" and "your confidence soon flower" as well as "you've lost your", the I sound in "light shines", the A sound in "blackest day".

Consonance: the P sound in "up hope", the L sound in "will flower" and "you'll learn", the S sounds in "as stumble darkness".

Caesura: line 1, line 12, line 19.

This picture is of the tunnel along the Bruce Vento Pathway that creates the bridge for 7th street as it runs from the sandstone bluffs, known as Dayton's Bluff, over the railroad tracks and into downtown St. Paul. It was taken in March, 2012. The picture moved me to write this poem.

CHAPTER 6: SCENES

"What are Scenes?", you might ask.

For the purposes of this book, scenes are poems based on a photograph that says something. It can be an event, or an image that moves you in some way. The purpose of the poem is for the poet to convey the meaning or feeling that speaks to him. Hopefully, it connects with the reader too in that way.

Poem #39:

AMERICA

(An Abecedarian)

America's history is filled with drama.
Beautiful sights leaves us numb.
Constitution laid ground for thoughts idyllic,
Developed dreams now abound.
Elemental free rights under which we live,
Freedom flies from every staff.

Generated the lifestyle we are living.
Healthy democratic worth,
Institutions libretti,
Juxtapositioned order against hadj padj,
Kingdom removed from our back,

Loosing new unbridled liberty for all.
Macro-evolution dream
Negated suggestion of hope's suppression.
Oppressive actions echo
Policy off the doorstep.

Quantified invention, like Twitter on BLAQ,
Revolution behavior,
Sensitized precedence of world governments
Through new ideas set aloft.
Union joined without adieu!

Viewed afar, our democratic POV,
With expectations anew,
Xenic thoughts create American tableaux.
Yankee found alacrity!
Zealouscy lit the passion, setting world abuzz.

I wrote this poem on 1/21/2013, inauguration day for President Obama. I thought it fitting. Although he was not my candidate, he is my President. His very election represents the diversity of our nation. This event represents the peaceful transition of power. The Martin Luther King holiday represents Civil rights and the abolition of slavery in the USA. I hope this poem carries some of that through it.

This is an Alphabet Poem within an Abcedarian Poem. The highlighted first words in blue reading down the page are a poem within the poem.

In addition, the last letter in every line of the Abcedarian is the same letter of the alphabet as the starting word, usually in lower case where possible.

The syllable count for this poem is as follows: 11-7-11-7-11-7, 11-7-7, 11-7-11-7-11-7-7, 11-7-11-7-7. 11-7-11-7-11.

Color scheme: red, white, and blue

An Abecdarian Poem, is a poem using the 26 letters of the alphabet chronologically. It is a special form of an Acrostic poem, in which the initial letters of the words begin each line or stanza spell out the alphabet in order.

An Alphabet Poem is the same, only the lines consist of a single word starting with each letter of the Alphabet in chronological sequence.

Alacrity: enjoyment

BLAQ: an APP that carries Twitter on Blackberries

Hadj Padj: I found this in scrabble - older English for Hodge Podge, disorderly.

Libretti: operatic, with musical drama.

Juxtapositioned: laid side by side, to examine.

Macro-evolution: evolving from within.

Precedence: what has been established or gone before.

POV: Point of View.

Sensitized: made aware of.

Tableaux: striking, dramatic scene.

Xenic: foreign.

Zealouscy: Having much zeal or energy.

Alliteration: developed dreams, freedom flies, loosing liberty.

In-line Rhyme: hadj padj

This photograph was taken by the author in a parking lot at Pipestone, Minnesota in August, 2012.

Poem #40:

CASTING SHADOWS
(A Lisalet Poem)

I delight in sunlight casting shadows,
On a warm sunny summer afternoon.
It's amazing, when that golden orb glows,
Then hard objects get their images strewn.

On a warm sunny summer afternoon,
I love to sit and watch the dark sideshows
On the ground that such sights festoon.
I delight in sunlight casting shadows.

It's amazing, when that golden orb glows,
All the shapes and images that get hewn.
'Cause Earth's a canvas where the sun's ray goes
On a warm sunny summer afternoon.

Then hard objects get their images strewn
In fragile formats that the light bestows.
Watchers don't want the scene to end too soon.
It's amazing, when that golden orb glows.

On a warm sunny summer afternoon,
I delight in sunlight casting shadows.

Sidewalk shadows of tables and grass on a sunny day. I just liked the image. Especially the table legs. This picture inspired the poem.

This poem is a Lisalet.

Lisalet Poem: a style created by Lisa Sherman on FanStory, that has a fixed format of repeating lines and, when rhymed, a forced set of only two rhyme choices in an abab rhyme scheme.

The format repeats the first four lines in a structured, reverse cascade down the stanzas as follows:

1/2/3/4 2/5/6/1 3/7/8/2 4/9/10/3, such that the stanzas incorporate the repeating lines as 1/2 2/1 3/2 4/3 (I added also a closing 2/1) as the first and last lines of each stanza. The optional rhyme scheme becomes A1,B1,A2,B2 B1,a,b,A1 A2,b,a,B2 B2,a,b,A2. The capitals represent the repeated lines. I hope that all makes sense.

I chose the syllable count to be 10, but that is not a requirement. I also added a closing couplet using B1,A1, but that is not a requirement either.

Alliteration: sunny summer, golden glows, such sights, 'cause canvas, fragile formats, watchers want, scene soon.

Assonance: the O sound in "golden orb glows".

Consonance: the Ts in "sit watch", the S sound in "sunlight casting shadows", the Gs in "images get", the T sounds in "formats that the light bestows" and in "watchers don't want the to too".

Caesura: line 3, line 9, line 16.

In-line Rhyme: delight sunlight.

This photograph was taken by the author himself at a Bruegger's coffee shop in Woodbury, Minnesota.

Poem #41:

CHERUB FOUNTAIN

(A Rondeau Redouble)

Yon cherubs dance delightfully in sky.
These little water nymphs pleasantly play
On marble pool, perched with grace and placed high,
Attracting attention of passersby.

Below, demons that spew water away,
Depict that opposing forces apply,
As heaven's offset with hellish display.
Yon cherubs dance delightfully in sky!

Under where whiskered beasts wistfully try
To fill up fine pool with fish fluid spray,
With Earth's seas beneath, above keeping dry,
These little water nymphs pleasantly play.

The water flows forth, recycling all day
Inside park, where it makes people sigh,
They cavort in naked glee, as they may,
On marble pool, perched with grace and placed high.

The sunlight glistens off each silver ray
That arcs to pool as sparkling droplets fly.
A fountain display that's a touch risque,
Attracting attention of passersby.

Many levels of purpose underlie
Three cosmic sites shown in artistic array.
As Heaven, Hell, and Earth, they signify.
I'd venture to see it without delay.

Yon cherubs dance!

I went over to Lake Harriet in Minneapolis the other day. It has a fabulous Rose Garden there. In it is this magnificent water fountain. At the top are seven naked cherubs cavorting in a large marble bowl that spills down into a pool. Below them are demons with horns and goatees spewing water into clam shells, as underneath sea monsters with mustached whiskers blow water from their mouths into the pool below. So this artistic fountain represents heaven, hell, and the sea covered earth. I was moved by the site to write this poem.

The poem is a Rondeau Redouble. It is a poem with a very complex fixed format. It is written on two rhymes (the a and b rhymes), but in five stanzas of four lines each and one of five lines that repeats a portion of the first line of the poem.

Each of the first four lines (which due to the a and b rhymes will be identified in the following stanzas as A1, B1, A2 and B2) get individually repeated in turn once in the following stanzas by becoming successively the respective fourth lines of stanzas 2, 3, 4, & 5; and the first part of the first line is repeated as a short fifth line to conclude the sixth stanza. The stanzas each carry an abab rhyme scheme, so with the repeat line shown in numbered capitals, this can be represented as - A1,B1,A2,B2 - b,a,b,A1 - a,b,a,B1 - b,a,b,A2 - a,b,a,B2 - b,a,b,a,(A1).

This poem can have any meter. For this poem I chose iambic pentameter, which has lines that have 10 syllables and a tempo of: da-Dum da-Dum da-Dum da-Dum da-Dum.

Alliteration: dance delightfully, pleasantly play, pool perched placed, attracting attention, heaven's hellish, dance delightfully, whiskered wistfully, fill fine fish fluid, flows forth, park people, sites shown, artistic array, Heaven hell.

This photograph was taken by the author himself.

Poem #42:

EVERGREEN
(5-7-5 Poem)

Pines are evergreen
So it was to my surprise
I learned otherwise

Was walking in the woods the other day and came across this burst of color that was reminiscent of autumn. It was just this dying pine tree. I took its picture and it inspired this little poem. Not always evergreen, are they?

This poem is a simple 5-7-5 Poem.

A 5-7-5 is the American version of a Japanese Haiku.

It is written in 3 lines.

Line 1: 5 syllables

Line 2: 7 syllables

Line 3: 5 syllables

Rhyming not required.

I did rhyme line 2 and 3.

Alliteration: so surprise.

Assonance: the E sounds in "learned otherwise".

Consonance: the S sound in "was surprise", the R sound in "learned otherwise" the N sound in "pines evergreen.

Poem #43:

FIDO ON THE ROOF
(ABAB Quatrains)

Looked across the street this morning,
There was a doggy on the roof.
The surprise came without warning
When I was startled by a "woof".

Upon the neighbor's garage top,
High up in winter's frozen air,
Dog was examining the drop.
Knew he shouldn't be up there.

Now, how did it get up there?
I don't think anybody knows.
I've seen it there before, I swear,
It seems to happen when it snows.

Though it really is amazing,
He could be caught up there all day.
Judging noises he is raising,
It's quite a scary place to stay.

It surpasses understanding
That his down exit could be rough.
It could be a nasty landing,
If he decided to hop off.

So if you spot that doggy, don't give me any guff.
Run and get a ladder, he's been up there long enough!

This is a true story. My neighbor across the street from me has a dog that climbs up on the roof. He jumps from the top of his dog house, to the top of a storage shed, then up to the roof. It startled me the first time I saw him, and it was in the wintertime.

This poem is a simple set of abab rhyming quatrains in tetrameter.

Alliteration: without warning, when was woof, dog drop, seems snows, could caught, scary stay, doggy don't, ladder long.

Assonance: the O sounds in "looked across morning" and "doggy roof", also "upon neighbor's top", the E sound in "he be there", the Es in "seen there before swear", the U and S sounds in "surpasses understanding", the OU in "could rough", the A sound in "nasty landing". The O sounds in "to hop off".

Consonance: the N sound in "don't think anybody", the Z sound in "is amazing", the S sound in "noises is raising", the T sounds in " it's quite stay", the C in "scary place", and the G sound in "long enough".

Caesura: line 9, line 11, line 21, line 22.

Onomatopoeia: woof.

In-line Rhyme: Now how, there swear.

I took that picture 3/6/2013, after I finished shoveling.

Poem #44:

GO FLY A KITE
(5-7-5 Suite)

Family with the kite
Here within the field of sight
Sharing their delight

Feelings touching sky
Running free their spirits fly
As their kite climbs high

Floating in the air
Precious family time they share
Joy without a care

Sharing happiness
Is one secret to success
Life that God will bless

Family in the field flying a kite. The scene of family togetherness created the feeling expressed in this poem.

The poem is a suite of 4 related 5-7-5 Poems.

A 5-7-5 formatted poem is an American version of the Japanese Haiku, only without all the formal requirements of a Haiku.

As such it contains only 3 lines designated by their syllable count.

Line 1: 5 syllables

Line 2: 7 syllables

Line 3: 5 Syllables

No rhyme or meter required. I mono-rhymed this one in each stanza.

Alliteration: free fly, secret success, time they.

Assonance: the ING sound in "feelings touching", the I sound in "in Air".

Consonance: the T sound in "with kite", the R sound in "sharing there", the K sound in "kite climbs", the M sound in "family time".

This photograph was taken at Battle Creek Park, in Maplewood, Minnesota.

Poem #45:

QUIET SOLITUDE

(Tercets)

I often go to the park
In Afternoon
Or after dark

I seek out serenity
Upon a seat
Under a tree

With nature all around me
Clean air I breathe
My mind can see

In the Quiet Solitude
I want to be
My soul's set free

Going to the park can be a spiritual experience. What is closer to God than a Cathedral of trees?

This poem rhymes the first and last lines of each tercet, except the last, which rhymes the last two.

The syllable count for each is 7,4,4.

Alliteration: seek serenity, all around, my mind, soul's set.

Assonance: the O sound in "often go to", the A sound in "after dark" and "nature all", the EA sounds in "clean breathe", and the E sound in "set free".

Consonance: the N sounds in "in afternoon" and "mind can", the R sounds in "or after dark", the T sound in "out serenity" and quiet solitude".

When I took this photograph in January 2012, it spoke the words to me "Quiet Solitude" immediately. I've looked at it many times since with the same thought. If you look closely there is a man sitting on a bench reading among the trees. Today, a year later, I finally got around to writing the poem that I always meant to write.

This photograph is the reason that this poem exists, it moved my Muse to express what I saw in verse.

Poem #46:

SPLISH SPLASH
(Free Style)

Splish Splash
as
rain drops dash
upon the ice
they cut and gash
Winter
away.

~

Hurray!

><

This is a picture of rain drops falling onto an ice mound, forming a puddle that is cutting it away as the rain continues to fall.

This is a Free Style Poem.

A Free Style Poem is a subset of Free Verse. It has no rhyme scheme or meter pattern. It just flows with the words. The author adds dimension in how the poem is felt, through the use of pace and pause, created in how the words are arranged on the page. The distinction between Free Style and Free Verse is that Free Style contains some rhyme while Free Verse does not. It rhymes in places as the author wants, but not necessarily consistently.

Alliteration: splish splash, drops dash.

Assonance: the A sounds in "as rain dash".

Consonance: the S sounds in "splish splash as", the R sound in "rain drops", the W sound in "winter away".

Onomatopoeia: splish splash.

The photograph was taken by me on March 30, 2013. Rain was melting off my roof and dropping into puddles. I tried to catch the action of the drops.

Poem #47:

TANGLED, TORN, AND TWISTED
(Sestet)

Abandoned and forgotten along the road,
Beside a field no longer sowed,
Above the gnarled growth, it rises high,
A darkened silhouette in the sky.
From its strong blades once water flowed
- But that was in the days gone by.

Today it stands there tangled and torn;
Dismissed, forgotten, abandoned, forlorn.
Its blades are broken, lost and scattered.
Its former proud history hasn't mattered.
It's choked in vines, covered in thorn
- It stands there weathered, beaten, battered.

I was out there on that forgotten road,
Beside that field no longer sowed.
I almost passed it, but I resisted.
An opportunity to capture it existed,
Of a weathered windmill that really showed
- A structure tangled, torn, and twisted.

When driving down country roads you can't help but see fallow fields, decaying barns, and sad symbols of better times. They provide stunning images of what once was. This is a photograph I took in the Afton area of Minnesota. It is a good example. Hopefully there are better times ahead.

This poem is a Sestet. It is a poem that has 6 lines. Basically, it's just a categorical designation. It can have no, or any, rhyme scheme. There is no specific requirement for meter,

For this poem, I did use a rhyme scheme,

The rhyme scheme is: aabbab.

I wrote it with mixed meter.

Alliteration: gnarled growth, silhouette sky, tangled torn twisted, forgotten forlorn, blades broken, history hasn't, choked covered, beaten battered, out on, weathered windmill.

Assonance: the O in "abandoned forgotten along road" and "no longer sowed", the I sound in "rises high", the Y sound in "days by", the Os in forgotten abandoned forlorn, the EA sound in "weathered really".

Consonance: the N sounds in "abandoned forgotten along road" and "no longer sowed", the W sound in "once water flowed", the T sound in "today it stands there tangled torn", the V sound in "vines covered", the N sound in "in thorn", the T sounds in "out there that forgotten", the S sound in "almost passed resisted", the T sounds in "opportunity to capture it existed".

Caesura: line 3, line 8, line 9, line 11, line 12, line 15, line 18.

This photograph was taken by the author in November, 2012.

Poem #48:

THE BIKE

(A Modified Tyburn)

Unique
and chic
It's bold
It's gold
It's bold! It's gold! So who wouldn't like
To shine on this unique and chic bike?

This bike was spotted at a car show that I attended in August, 2012. Finally got around to writing a poem for this photograph.

This poem is a modified Tyburn.

Tyburn: A six line poem consisting of 2, 2, 2, 2, 9, 9 fixed syllables.

The first four lines rhyme and are all descriptive words. The last two lines rhyme and incorporate the first, second, third, and fourth lines as the 5th through 8th syllables.

Syllable Count

line 1 - 2 syllables.
line 2 - 2 syllables.
line 3 - 2 syllables.
line 4 - 2 syllables.
line 5 - 9 syllables.
line 6 - 9 syllables.

Rhyme scheme: aabbcc

The reason this is called a "modified" Tyburn is because I didn't follow the syllable 5th through 8th syllable requirement, but rather incorporated lines 1 to 4 within both line 5 and 6. Done intentionally and so noted.

Alliteration: who wouldn't.

Assonance: the O sounds in "bold gold so who wouldn't".

Consonance: the N sound in "shine on unique".

In-line Rhyme: the poems very format requires forced in-line rhyming on lines 5 and 6.

Caesura: line 5 and 6.

This photo was taken by the author himself at the Woodbury, Minnesota location just off of I-494 and Valley Creek Roads.

Poem #49:

THE POND

(Free Verse)

As I went down a path
surrounded
shoulder to shoulder
by
caressing greenery,
I heard the gentle
dribbling
of flowing water.
I glimpsed color
through the foilage
from time to time.

Then I turned a corner
and
beheld
a wooden bench
beside the sparkling water.

I turned again
and
there before me
was
a lovely pond
with a water fountain.
It teamed with
beautiful
Koi
and left me
with
a feeling of

Peace and Joy

The Marguary McNeely Conservatory at the Como Zoo in St. Paul, Minnesota has a room full of ferns. It's a beautiful room where you wind your way around aisles of exotic plants. Its a wonderful place to visit on a cold snowy Minnesota winter's day. You walk through a maze shoulder to shoulder through dense foliage with lush tropical plants. In the center of that room is a lovely pond. This photograph is the reason that this poem exists, it moved my Muse to express what I saw in verse. It inspired me to write this poem.

Koi are colorful fish that are very similar in shape to large goldfish, only with variegated colors. I have a picture of them in a poem named Koi.

This poem is Free Verse.

Free Verse poetry is a very open and free flowing form of poetry written without required formats. There is no fixed meter, tempo, or rhyme. The author, instead, paints a poetic picture with the words. The author adds dimension in how the poem is felt, through the use of pace and pause, created in how the words are arranged on the page. This can create very moving thoughts and images. Done correctly, it can turn simple sentences into lovely works of art.

Alliteration: In a Free Verse poem you judge alliteration not by line (which can be just one word), but by phrases. In this poem it is: surrounded shoulder shoulder, foliage from, time time, then turned, beheld bench beside, again and, with water.

Assonance: the A sounds in "as a path", the O sounds in "color through foliage" and "lovely pond", the E sound in "caressing greenery" and "wooden bench".

Consonance: the W in "flowing water", the T sounds in "water fountain" and in "it teamed with beautiful", and also "left with", the F sound in "feeling of". The L sounds in "gentle flowing glimpsed color foliage".

Onomatopoeia: dribbling

I took this photograph shown here in the Conservatory of the center pond area on a March morning in 2012.

Poem #50:

THIS WALL, THIS FALL
(Momo-rhyme Poem)

As I wandered on a walk this fall,
I came across this mortised wall,
Capped with stones both large and small.
Above It spread the season's shawl
Of leaves so rich the colors call.

It wasn't tall, as I recall.
Below it, the leaf strewn path was small,
With ground coverage enough to have a ball
When kids go kick, and jump and sprawl.

I was blessed to find this wall this fall,
To walk the path, to see it all,
And what I thought was best of all
Were those colors that kept me in their thrall.

As a walked along the sidewalk this fall kicking leaves and marveling at the colors, I came upon this lovely low wall that I photographed. It inspired me to write this poem - a picture Poem, if you will.

This poem is a Mono-rhyme Poem.

A Mono-rhyme poem is a poem that has the same end rhyme. The rhyme may be within a stanza, or throughout the entire poem, like this one has three mono rhymed stanzas. All of the stanzas use the same end-rhyme.

Alliteration: wandered walk, spread season's shawl, colors call, strewn small, kids kick, and and, what was, those that their thrall.

Assonance: the A sounds in "as wandered a walk fall", the IS sound in "this mortised", the O sounds in "stones both" and "of so colors" as well as "ground coverage enough to", the E sounds in "below the leaf strewn".

Consonance: the C sound in "came across", the T sound in "it wasn't tall" and "to the path to it", the Ws in "when sprawl", the S sounds in "was blessed this this".

In-line Rhyme: tall recall, wall fall.

Caesura: line 6, line 7, line 9, line 11.

This photograph was taken by the author in October, 2012.

GLOSSARY OF POETRY TYPES